Guided Reading and Study

From Bacteria to Plants

PRENTICE HALL **Science** Explorer

PEARSON

Prentice Hall

Boston, Massachusetts
Upper Saddle River, New Jersey

Copyright © by Pearson Education, Inc., publishing as Pearson Prentice Hall, Boston, Massachusetts 02116. All rights reserved. Printed in the United States of America. This publication is protected by copyright, and permission should be obtained from the publisher prior to any prohibited reproduction, storage in a retrieval system, or transmission in any form or by any means, electronic, mechanical, photocopying, recording, or likewise. The publisher hereby grants permission to reproduce these pages, in part or in whole, for classroom use only, the number not to exceed the number of students in each class. Notice of copyright must appear on all copies. For information regarding permission(s), write to: Rights and Permissions Department, One Lake Street, Upper Saddle River, NJ 07458.

Pearson Prentice Hall™ is a trademark of Pearson Education, Inc.
Pearson® is a registered trademark of Pearson plc.
Prentice Hall® is a registered trademark of Pearson Education, Inc.

ISBN 0-13-190168-0   9 10   09 08

From Bacteria to Plants

© Pearson Education, Inc., publishing as Pearson Prentice Hall. All rights reserved.

🔥 Target Reading Skills

Identifying Main Ideas

Identifying the main idea helps you understand what you are reading. Sometimes the main idea can be easy to find. For example, suppose that you are reading just one paragraph. Very often you will find the main idea in the first sentence, the topic sentence. The other sentences in the paragraph provide supporting details or support the ideas in the topic sentence.

Sometimes, however, the first sentence is not the topic sentence. Sometimes you may have to look further. In those cases, it might help to read the paragraph and summarize what you have read. Your summary can give you the main idea.

A textbook has many paragraphs, each one with its own main idea. However, just as a paragraph has a main idea and supporting details, so does the text under each heading in your textbook. Sometimes the main idea is the heading itself. Other times it is more difficult to find. You may have to infer a main idea by combining information from several paragraphs.

To practice this skill, you can use a graphic organizer that looks like this one.

Main Idea		
Detail	**Detail**	**Detail**
a.	b.	c.

Outlining

Outlining shows you how supporting details relate to main ideas. You can make an outline as you read. Using this skill can make you a more careful reader.

Your outline can be made up of sentences, simple phrases, or single words. What matters is that you follow a formal structure. To outline while you read, use a plan like this one.

I. Section Title
   A. Main Heading
      1. Subheading
         a. Detail
         b. Detail
         c. Detail

The main ideas or topics are labeled as Roman numerals. The supporting details or subtopics are labeled A, B, C, and so on. Other levels of supporting information can be added under heads. When you outline in this way, you are deciding just how important a piece of information is.

© Pearson Education, Inc., publishing as Pearson Prentice Hall. All rights reserved.

Science Explorer ▪ *Target Reading Skills Handbook*

Comparing and Contrasting

You can use comparing and contrasting to better understand similarities and differences between two or more concepts. Look for clue words as you read. When concepts or topics are similar, you will probably see words such as *also, just as, like, likewise,* or *in the same way.* When concepts or topics are different, you will see *but, however, although, whereas, on the other hand,* or *unlike.*

To use this skill, it sometimes helps to make a Venn diagram. In this type of graphic organizer, the similarities are in the middle, where the two circles overlap.

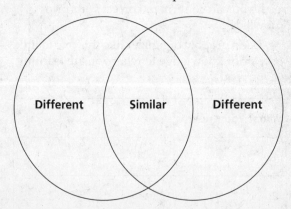

Relating Cause and Effect

Identifying causes and effects can help you understand the relationships among events. A cause is what makes something happen. An effect is what happens. In science, many actions cause other actions to occur.

Sometimes you have to look hard to see a cause-and-effect relationship in reading. You can watch for clue words to help you identify causes and effects. Look for *because, so, since, therefore, results, cause,* or *lead to.*

Sometimes a cause-and-effect relationship occurs in a chain. For example, an effect can have more than one cause, or a cause can have several effects. Seeing and understanding the relationships helps you understand science processes. You can use a graphic organizer like this one.

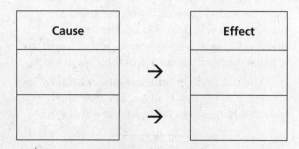

Asking Questions

Your textbook is organized using headings and subheadings. You can read the material under those headings by turning each heading into a question. For example, you might change the heading "Protecting Yourself During an Earthquake" to "How can you protect yourself during an earthquake?" Asking questions in this way will help you look for answers while reading. You can use a graphic organizer like this one to ask questions.

Question	Answer

© Pearson Education, Inc., publishing as Pearson Prentice Hall. All rights reserved.

Name _____ Date _____ Class _____

Sequencing

Sequencing is the order in which a series of events occurs. As you read, look for clue words that tell you the sequence or the order in which things happen. You see words such as *first, next, then,* or *finally*. When a process is being described, watch for numbered steps. Sometimes there are clues provided for you. Using the sequencing reading skill will help you understand and visualize the steps in a process. You can also use it to list events in the order of their occurrence.

You can use a graphic organizer to show the sequence of events or steps. The one most commonly used is a flowchart like this one.

Sometimes, though, a cycle diagram works better.

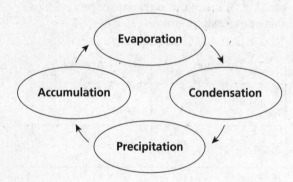

Using Prior Knowledge

Use prior knowledge to relate what you are reading to something that you already know. It is easier to learn when you can link new ideas to something that is already familiar to you. For example, if you know that fish are actually breathing oxygen that is dissolved in water, you wil be able to understand how or why gills work.

Using prior knowledge can help you make logical assumptions or draw conclusions about what you are reading. But be careful. Your prior knowledge might sometimes be wrong. As you read, you can confirm or correct your prior knowledge.

Use a graphic organizer like this one to link your prior knowledge to what you are learning as you read.

What You Know
1.
2.
3.

What You Learned
1.
2.
3.

© Pearson Education, Inc., publishing as Pearson Prentice Hall. All rights reserved.

Science Explorer ▪ *Target Reading Skills Handbook*

Previewing Visuals

Looking at visuals before you read can help you better understand a topic. Preview the visuals by reading labels and captions. For example, if you preview the visuals in a chapter about volcanoes, you will see more than just photographs of erupting volcanoes. You will see maps, diagrams, and photographs of rocks. These might tell you that you will learn where volcanoes are found, how they form, and what sort of rock is created when volcanoes erupt. Previewing visuals helps you understand and enjoy what you read.

One way to apply this strategy is to choose a few photographs, diagrams, or other visuals to preview. Then write questions about what you see. Answer the questions as you read.

Identifying Supporting Evidence

In science, you will read about hypotheses. A hypothesis is a possible explanation for scientific observations made by scientists or an answer to a scientific question. A hypothesis is tested over and over again. The tests may produce evidence that supports the hypothesis. When enough supporting evidence is collected, a hypothesis may become a theory.

Identifying supporting evidence in your reading can help you understand a hypothesis or theory. Evidence is made up of facts. Facts are information that can be confirmed by testing or observation.

When you are identifying supporting evidence, a graphic organizer like this one can be helpful.

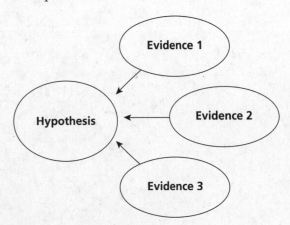

Building Vocabulary

To understand what someone is saying, you have to know the language that person is speaking. To understand science, you need to know what the words mean.

There are many ways to build your vocabulary. You can look up the meaning of a new word in a dictionary or glossary. Then you can write its definition in your own words. You can use the new word in a sentence. To figure out the meaning of a new word, you can use context clues or surrounding words. Look for prefixes and suffixes in the new word to help you break it down. Building vocabulary will get easier with practice.

© Pearson Education, Inc., publishing as Pearson Prentice Hall. All rights reserved.

Name _____ Date _____ Class _____

Living Things ▪ *Guided Reading and Study*

What Is Life? (pp. 6–14)

This section explains the characteristics of living things and what living things need to survive.

Use Target Reading Skills

Look at the section headings and visuals to see what this section is about. Then write what you already know about living things in the graphic organizer below. As you read, write what you learn.

What You Know
1. Living things grow.
2.

What You Learned
1.
2.

The Characteristics of Living Things (pp. 7–9)

1. What is an organism?

_____

_____

© Pearson Education, Inc., publishing as Pearson Prentice Hall. All rights reserved.

Living Things ▪ *Guided Reading and Study*

What Is Life? *(continued)*

2. List six characteristics that all living things share.

    a. _____

    b. _____

    c. _____

    d. _____

    e. _____

    f. _____

3. The basic building blocks of all organisms are _____ .

4. Is the following sentence true or false? Most cells can be seen only with a microscope, a tool that magnifies small objects. _____

5. Is the following sentence true or false? An organism made of many cells is a unicellular organism. _____

6. Circle the letter of the most abundant chemical in cells.

    a. proteins
    b. carbohydrates
    c. water
    d. nucleic acids

7. Lipids and _____ are the building materials of cells.

8. Is the following sentence true or false? The cells of organisms use energy for growth and repair. _____

9. Circle the letter of a change in an organism's surroundings that causes the organism to react.

    a. growth
    b. response
    c. stimulus
    d. development

© Pearson Education, Inc., publishing as Pearson Prentice Hall. All rights reserved.

Living Things • *Guided Reading and Study*

10. Give one example of a stimulus and one example of a response.

    Stimulus: _____

    Response: _____

11. What is development?

    _____

    _____

    _____

12. All organisms can _____, or produce offspring that are similar to the parents.

Life Comes From Life (pp. 10–11)

13. Is the following sentence true or false? Flies can arise from rotting meat.

    _____

14. The idea that living things can come from nonliving sources is called

    _____.

15. What did Francesco Redi show in his experiment?

    _____

    _____

    _____

    _____

16. The factor that a scientist changes in a controlled experiment is the _____

    _____.

17. Is the following sentence true or false? Louis Pasteur used a controlled experiment to show that bacteria arise from spontaneous generation.

    _____

© Pearson Education, Inc., publishing as Pearson Prentice Hall. All rights reserved.

Name _____ Date _____ Class _____

What Is Life? *(continued)*

The Needs of Living Things (pp. 12–14)

18. Complete this concept map to show what living things need to survive.

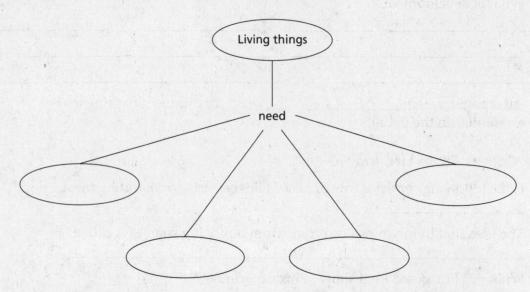

19. Is the following sentence true or false? Living things use food as their energy source to carry out their life functions. _____

20. Organisms that make their own food are called _____.
    Organisms that cannot make their own food are called _____
    _____.

21. Is the following sentence true or false? Living things can live without water for long periods of time. _____

22. Why do living things need water?

    _____

    _____

    _____

23. Is the following sentence true or false? Organisms compete with each other for space to live. _____

24. Why must living things have homeostasis, or stable internal conditions?

    _____

    _____

© Pearson Education, Inc., publishing as Pearson Prentice Hall. All rights reserved.

Living Things · *Guided Reading and Study*

Classifying Organisms (pp. 16–24)

This section tells how scientists divide living things into groups. It also describes the first classification systems and how the theory of evolution changed classification systems.

Use Target Reading Skills

Before you read, preview the red headings. In the graphic organizer below, ask a what, why, or how question for each heading. As you read, write the answers to your questions.

Classifying Organisms

Question	Answer
Why do scientists classify?	Scientists classify because...

© Pearson Education, Inc., publishing as Pearson Prentice Hall. All rights reserved.

Living Things • *Guided Reading and Study*

Classifying Organisms *(continued)*

Why Do Scientists Classify? (p. 17)

1. The process of grouping things based on their similarities is

   _____.

2. Why do biologists use classification?

   _____

   _____

   _____

3. The scientific study of how living things are classified is called

   _____.

4. Is the following sentence true or false? Once an organism is classified, a scientist knows a lot about that organism. _____

The Naming System of Linnaeus (pp. 18–19)

5. Is the following sentence true or false? Linnaeus placed organisms into groups based on their features that he could observe.

   _____

6. In Linnaeus's naming system, called _____, each organism is given a two-part name.

7. Is the following sentence true or false? A species is a group of similar organisms that can mate with each other and produce offspring that can also mate and reproduce. _____

8. *Felis concolor* is the scientific name for mountain lions. To which genus do mountain lions belong? What is the species?

   Genus: _____ Species: _____

9. Circle the letter of each sentence that is true about binomial nomenclature.

   a. A scientific name is written in italics.
   b. Many scientific names are in Latin because Latin was the language of scientists during Linnaeus's time.
   c. The genus name begins with a small letter.
   d. Binomial nomenclature makes it easy for scientists to talk about an organism.

© Pearson Education, Inc., publishing as Pearson Prentice Hall. All rights reserved.

Living Things · *Guided Reading and Study*

Levels of Classification (pp. 20–21)

10. List the eight levels of classification used by modern biologists in order from the broadest level to the most specific level.

_____

_____

_____

11. Is the following sentence true or false? The more classification levels that two organisms share, the more characteristics they have in common.

_____

12. Look carefully at the figure, *Levels of Classification*, in your textbook. What order does the great horned owl belong to?

_____

_____

Taxonomic Keys (p. 22)

13. Name two ways to learn the identity of an organism.

a. _____

b. _____

14. Is the following sentence true or false? A taxonomic key is a book with illustrations that highlight the differences between organisms that look similar. _____

15. Look at the taxonomic key in the figure, *Identifying Organisms*, in your textbook. How many legs does a tick have? _____

© Pearson Education, Inc., publishing as Pearson Prentice Hall. All rights reserved.

Living Things ▪ *Guided Reading and Study*

Classifying Organisms *(continued)*

Evolution and Classification *(pp. 23–24)*

16. Is the following sentence true or false? Darwin's theory of evolution did not affect the way in which species were classified. _____

17. What is evolution?

    _____

    _____

    _____

18. Is the following sentence true or false? Species with shared ancestors are classified more closely together. _____

19. What do scientists today rely on primarily to determine evolutionary history?

    _____

    _____

© Pearson Education, Inc., publishing as Pearson Prentice Hall. All rights reserved.

Name _____ Date _____ Class _____

Domains and Kingdoms (pp. 26–29)

This section describes each of the domains and kingdoms into which all living things are grouped.

Use Target Reading Skills

As you read, compare and contrast the characteristics of organisms in domains Bacteria, Archaea, and Eukarya by completing the table below.

Domain or Kingdom	Cell Type and Number	Able to Make Food?
Bacteria	Prokaryote; unicellular	
Archaea		
Eukarya: Protist		
Fungi		
Plants		
Animals		

1. List the three domains of living things.

   a. _____ b. _____

   c. _____

2. Complete the concept map to show how organisms are placed into domains and kingdoms.

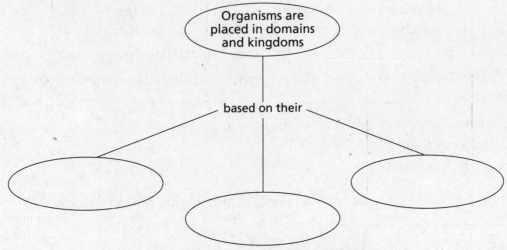

© Pearson Education, Inc., publishing as Pearson Prentice Hall. All rights reserved.

Living Things · *Guided Reading and Study*

Domains and Kingdoms (continued)

Domain Bacteria (p. 27)

3. Circle the letter of each sentence that is true about bacteria.

   a. Bacteria can be either autotrophic or heterotrophic.
   b. Bacteria are prokaryotes.
   c. Bacteria have a cell nucleus.
   d. Bacteria do not have nucleic acids.

4. A dense area in a cell that contains nucleic acids is a(n)

   _____.

Domain Archaea (p. 27)

5. Is the following sentence true or false? Archaea have a similar chemical makeup to bacteria. _____

6. Why are members of this domain called archaea, which comes from the Greek word for "ancient"?

   _____

   _____

Domain Eukarya (pp. 28–29)

7. Is the following sentence true or false? Protists can be either unicellular or multicellular. _____

8. How do protists differ from bacteria and archaea?

   _____

   _____

   _____

9. Is the following sentence true or false? Mushrooms, molds, mildew, and yeast are all fungi. _____

10. Circle the letter of each characteristic of fungi.

    a. eukaryotes   **c.** autotrophs
    b. prokaryotes   **d.** heterotrophs

11. Plants are _____; they can make their own food.

12. Is the following true or false? Plants provide food for all the heterotrophs on Earth. _____

13. Circle the letter of each characteristic of animals.

    a. unicellular   **c.** eukaryotes
    b. heterotrophs   **d.** autotrophs

14. Is the following sentence true or false? All animals are multicellular.

    _____

© Pearson Education, Inc., publishing as Pearson Prentice Hall. All rights reserved.

Living Things • *Guided Reading and Study*

The Origin of Life (pp. 30–33)

This section describes how Earth's atmosphere formed and how scientists think life first appeared on Earth.

Use Target Reading Skills

As you read, identify the evidence that supports scientists' hypothesis of how life arose on Earth. Write the evidence in the graphic organizer below.

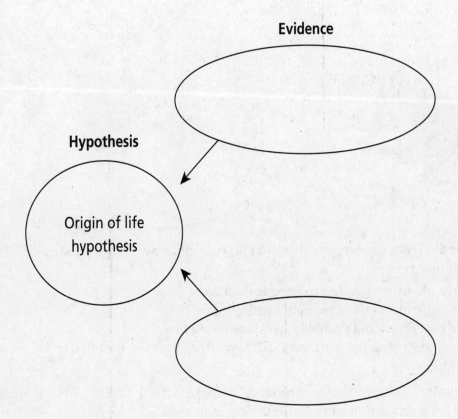

© Pearson Education, Inc., publishing as Pearson Prentice Hall. All rights reserved.

Living Things · *Guided Reading and Study*

The Origin of Life *(continued)*

The Atmosphere of Early Earth *(pp. 30–31)*

1. Complete this Venn diagram to compare the major gases that made up early Earth's atmosphere and Earth's atmosphere today.

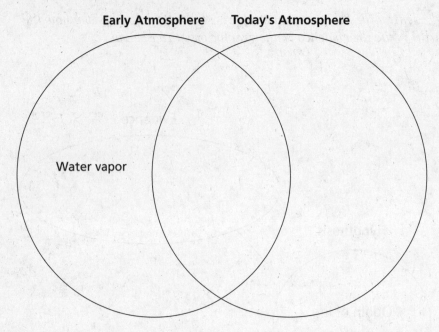

Early Atmosphere   Today's Atmosphere

Water vapor

2. Circle the letter of each sentence that is true about the characteristics of Earth's early life forms.

   a. Early life forms needed oxygen to survive.
   b. Early life forms were probably unicellular.
   c. The first life forms probably lived in the oceans.
   d. The first organisms were very different from archaea that live today in extreme conditions.

3. Is the following sentence true or false? Scientists think that the first life forms on Earth probably did arise from nonliving materials. _____

4. What materials did Stanley Miller and Harold Urey use to recreate the conditions of early Earth in their laboratory?

   _____

   _____

   _____

5. Miller and Urey used an electric current in their experiment to simulate

   _____ .

© Pearson Education, Inc., publishing as Pearson Prentice Hall. All rights reserved.

Living Things ▪ *Guided Reading and Study*

6. What were the results of Miller and Urey's experiment?

_____

_____

_____

_____

The First Cells (pp. 32–33)

7. Scientists think that the small chemical units of life formed gradually over millions of years in Earth's _____.

8. Traces of ancient organisms that have been preserved in rock or other substances are _____.

9. Circle the letter before each sentence that is true about how life formed on Earth.
    a. Fossils show that archaea-like living things were on Earth between 3.4 and 3.5 billion years ago.
    b. The first cells probably used the chemicals in their surroundings for energy.
    c. Cells that made their own food produced oxygen as a waste product, which built up in Earth's atmosphere.
    d. Scientists know for certain how life first appeared on Earth.

© Pearson Education, Inc., publishing as Pearson Prentice Hall. All rights reserved.

Name _____ Date _____ Class _____

Living Things ▪ *Key Terms*

Key Terms

Use the clues to identify Key Terms from the chapter. Write the terms on the lines. Then find the words hidden in the puzzle and circle them. Words are across or up-and-down.

Clues	Key Terms
Change that produces a more complex organism	_____
A trace of an ancient organism that has been preserved in rock	_____
The maintenance of stable internal conditions	_____
A dense area in a cell that contains nucleic acids	_____
An organism whose cell lacks a nucleus	_____
A group of organisms that can mate and produce offspring that can also mate and reproduce	_____
Change in the surroundings that causes an organism to react	_____
The scientific study of how living things are classified	_____
The basic unit of structure and function in an organism	_____

```
e h p r o k a r y o t e j d e y v t a o

h s j i l f b t e h o m e o s t a s i s

d t l s k e t u h g d s m a e t b p u f

o i b p d e v e l o p m e n t f i n r f

a m p e o r d y w o v a r l t o c n y o

r u a c p j i o l g e r x d a v e m u s

p l n i s t w t a x o n o m y p l h r s

a u p e k t u o e d a s p u f c l v r i

h s i s h r a c v n u c l e u s m p r l
```

© Pearson Education, Inc., publishing as Pearson Prentice Hall. All rights reserved.

Viruses and Bacteria · *Guided Reading and Study*

Viruses (pp. 40–46)

This section describes what viruses are, what they look like, and how they multiply.

Use Target Reading Skills

As you read, make two flowcharts that show how active and hidden viruses multiply. Put the steps in the process in separate boxes in the flowchart in the order in which they occur.

How Active Viruses Multiply

Virus attaches to the surface of a living cell.

↓

Virus injects genetic material into cell

↓

↓

↓

How Hidden Viruses Multiply

↓

↓

↓

↓

© Pearson Education, Inc., publishing as Pearson Prentice Hall. All rights reserved.

Viruses and Bacteria ▪ *Guided Reading and Study*

Viruses *(continued)*

What Is a Virus? (pp. 41–42)

1. Why do biologists consider viruses to be nonliving?

   _____

   _____

   _____

2. Is the following sentence true or false? Viruses multiply the same way as other organisms. _____

3. Circle the name of a living thing that provides energy for a virus or an organism.

   a. parasite
   b. host
   c. bacteriophage
   d. particle

4. Viruses act like _____ because they destroy the cells in which they multiply.

5. What organisms can viruses infect?

   _____

   _____

6. Is the following sentence true or false? Each virus can enter only a few types of cells in a few specific species. _____

7. Is the following sentence true or false? All viruses have the same shape.

   _____

8. A virus that infects bacteria is called a(n) _____.

9. Is the following sentence true or false? Viruses are much smaller than bacteria. _____

10. Because viruses are so small, they are measured in units called

    _____.

11. How are viruses named?

    _____

12. Circle the letter of each sentence that is true about viruses.

    a. They are larger than cells.
    b. They need to be inside a living cell in order to reproduce.
    c. They can be named after people.
    d. They infect only animals.

© Pearson Education, Inc., publishing as Pearson Prentice Hall. All rights reserved.

Viruses and Bacteria ▪ *Guided Reading and Study*

The Structure of Viruses (p. 43)

13. Label the two basic parts of a virus in this diagram.

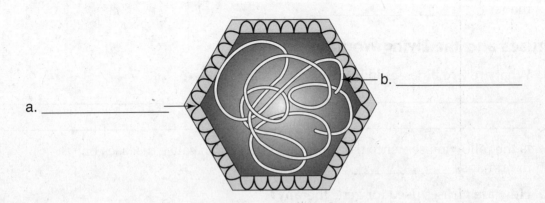

a. _____

b. _____

14. What are two functions of a virus's protein coat?

a. _____

b. _____

15. Is the following sentence true or false? The shape of the proteins allows the virus's coat to attach to only certain cells in the host.

_____

How Viruses Multiply (pp. 44–45)

Match the kind of virus with the way it multiplies in a cell. Viruses may be used more than once.

How It Multiplies

_____ **16.** The virus's genetic material becomes part of the cell's genetic material.

_____ **17.** The virus immediately begins to multiply after entering the cell.

_____ **18.** The virus stays inactive for a long time.

Viruses

a. active virus

b. hidden virus

© Pearson Education, Inc., publishing as Pearson Prentice Hall. All rights reserved.

Viruses and Bacteria ▪ *Guided Reading and Study*

Viruses *(continued)*

19. Is the following sentence true or false? When the virus is active, the cell makes the virus's proteins and genetic material and new viruses are made. _____

Viruses and the Living World (p. 46)

20. What are two illnesses in humans caused by viruses?

_____

_____

21. Is the following sentence true or false? Viruses can cause diseases only in humans. _____

22. How are viruses used for gene therapy?

_____

_____

_____

© Pearson Education, Inc., publishing as Pearson Prentice Hall. All rights reserved.

Viruses and Bacteria ▪ *Guided Reading and Study*

Bacteria (pp. 48–57)

This section explains what bacteria are, their positive roles, and how they reproduce.

Use Target Reading Skills

After you read the section, reread the paragraphs that contain definitions of Key Terms. Use all the information you have learned to write a definition of each Key Term in your own words.

The Bacterial Cell (pp. 48–49)

1. Bacteria are _____. The genetic material in their cells is not contained in a nucleus.

2. Is the following sentence true or false? Bacteria are living organisms because they use energy, grow, and respond to their surroundings.
    _____

3. What three shapes can bacterial cells have?

    a. _____ b. _____

    c. _____

4. Circle the letter of the cell structures where proteins are made.

    a. cell wall   b. cytoplasm
    c. ribosomes   d. flagellum

5. Label the parts of a bacterial cell in this diagram.

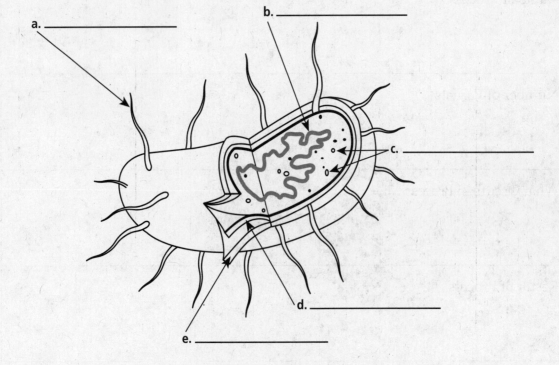

© Pearson Education, Inc., publishing as Pearson Prentice Hall. All rights reserved.

Viruses and Bacteria ▪ *Guided Reading and Study*

Bacteria *(continued)*

6. Is the following sentence true or false? Bacteria that do not have flagella are never moved from one place to another. _____

Obtaining Food and Energy (pp. 50–51)

7. List the two ways in which autotrophic bacteria make food.

   a. _____

   b. _____

8. How do heterotrophic bacteria get food?

   _____

   _____

9. Is the following sentence true or false? All bacteria must use oxygen to break down food for energy. _____

Reproduction (pp. 52–53)

10. Complete the table below about reproduction in bacteria.

Reproduction in Bacteria

	Asexual Reproduction	Sexual Reproduction
Name of Process		
Number of Parents		
What Occurs in Process		
Result of Process		

© Pearson Education, Inc., publishing as Pearson Prentice Hall. All rights reserved.

Name _____ Date _____ Class _____

Viruses and Bacteria • *Guided Reading and Study*

11. When do bacteria form endospores?

_____

_____

The Role of Bacteria in Nature (pp. 54–57)

12. Circle the letter of each sentence that is true about bacteria.

    a. All bacteria are harmful and cause disease.

    b. Some bacteria can use the sun's energy to make their own food.

    c. Bacteria help produce foods such as cheese, apple cider, and sauerkraut.

    d. Bacteria do not cause food to spoil.

13. Soil bacteria that break down large chemicals in dead organisms into small chemicals are called _____.

14. Is the following sentence true or false? Bacteria can be used to clean up oil spills and gasoline leaks. _____

15. List three ways that bacteria in your digestive system are helpful to you.

    a. _____

    b. _____

    c. _____

16. How do bacteria help people with diabetes?

_____

_____

_____

© Pearson Education, Inc., publishing as Pearson Prentice Hall. All rights reserved.

Viruses and Bacteria • *Guided Reading and Study*

Viruses, Bacteria, and Your Health (pp. 60–65)

This section explains how diseases are passed from person to person and how these diseases can be treated or prevented.

Use Target Reading Skills

Look at the section headings and visuals to see what this section is about. Then write what you already know about diseases caused by viruses and bacteria in the graphic organizer below. As you read, write what you learn.

What You Know
1. You can catch a cold from somebody who has one.
2.
3.

What You Learned
1.
2.
3.

How Infectious Diseases Spread (pp. 60–61)

1. What is an infectious disease?

    _____

    _____

    _____

© Pearson Education, Inc., publishing as Pearson Prentice Hall. All rights reserved.

Viruses and Bacteria • *Guided Reading and Study*

2. Complete this concept map to show how infectious diseases can spread.

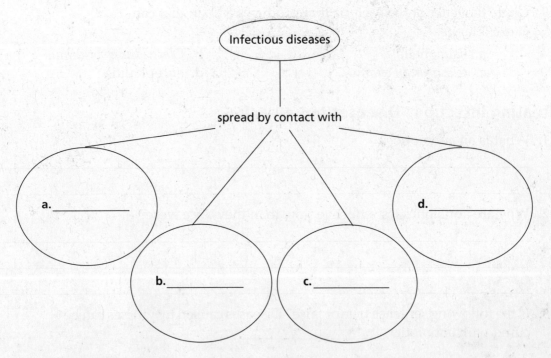

3. How do disease-causing agents enter the body?

_____

_____

_____

4. Is the following sentence true or false? The flu is spread only by direct contact, such as kissing a person with the flu. _____

5. Give one example of how objects can spread diseases.

_____

_____

_____

Match the animal with the disease that it spreads.

Disease	Animal
____ 6. rabies	a. ticks
____ 7. Lyme disease	b. raccoons
____ 8. encephalitis	c. mosquitoes

9. Is the following sentence true or false? Some viruses and bacteria that live in food, water, and soil can cause disease. _____

© Pearson Education, Inc., publishing as Pearson Prentice Hall. All rights reserved.

Viruses and Bacteria ▪ *Guided Reading and Study*

Viruses, Bacteria and Your Health *(continued)*

10. Circle the letter of the bacteria that produces a toxin that can cause tetanus.

      a. salmonella

      c. *Clostridium tetani*

      b. *Clostridium botulinum*

      d. encephalitis

Treating Infectious Diseases (pp. 62–64)

11. What is an antibiotic?

_____

_____

12. Why are antibiotics less effective now than they once were?

_____

_____

13. Is the following sentence true or false? Diseases caused by viruses can be cured with antibiotics. _____

Preventing Infectious Diseases (p. 65)

14. Is the following sentence true or false? A vaccine activates the body's natural defenses so that the body is ready to destroy an invading virus or bacterium. _____

15. What are three diseases that vaccines can protect you from?

_____

_____

16. Circle the letter of each sentence that is true about protecting yourself from infectious diseases.

      a. Eat nutritious food.

      b. Get plenty of rest, fluids, and exercise.

      c. Share eating utensils or cups.

      d. Get vaccinated.

17. What should you do if you get ill?

_____

_____

© Pearson Education, Inc., publishing as Pearson Prentice Hall. All rights reserved.

Viruses and Bacteria ▪ *Key Terms*

Key Terms

Use the clues below to identify Key Terms from the chapter. Write the terms on the lines, putting one letter in each blank. When you finish, the word enclosed in the diagonal lines will reveal the way in which bacteria multiply by asexual reproduction.

Clues

1. A virus that infects bacteria
2. Nonliving particle that invades cells
3. Two bacteria exchange genetic material
4. Harmful organism that lives on a host
5. Breaking down food to release energy
6. Region inside the cell membrane
7. Long, whiplike structure on bacteria

8. Chemical that kills only bacteria
9. Small, rounded, thick-walled, resting cell
10. Energy source for a parasite
11. Poison produced by bacteria
12. Cell part in which proteins are made
13. Stimulates the body to produce chemicals that destroy viruses and bacteria

1. _ _ _ _ _ _ _ _ _ _ _
2. _ _ _ _ _
3. _ _ _ _ _ _ _ _
4. _ _ _
5. _ _ _ _ _ _ _ _ _ _
6. _ _ _ _ _ _ _
7. _ _ _ _ _ _ _ _
8. _ _ _ _ _ _ _ _ _
9. _ _ _ _ _
10. _ _ _ _
11. _ _ _ _ _
12. _ _ _ _ _ _ _
13. _ _ _ _ _ _ _

© Pearson Education, Inc., publishing as Pearson Prentice Hall. All rights reserved.

Name _____ Date _____ Class _____

Protists and Fungi · *Guided Reading and Study*

Protists (pp. 74–83)

This section describes the characteristics of protists.

Use Target Reading Skills

As you read, make an outline about protists that you can use for review. Use the red section headings for the main topics and blue headings for the subtopics.

Protists

I. What is a protist?
II. Animal-like protists
    A. Protozoans with pseudopods
    B.
    C.
    D.
III.
    A.
    B.
    C.
    D.
    E.
    F.
IV.
    A.
    B.
    C.

What Is a Protist? (p. 75)

1. Circle the letter of each sentence that is true about protists.

    a. All protists are eukaryotes, organisms that have cells with nuclei.
    b. All protists live in dry surroundings.
    c. All protists are unicellular.
    d. Some protists are heterotrophs, some are autotrophs, and some are both.

© Pearson Education, Inc., publishing as Pearson Prentice Hall. All rights reserved.

Protists and Fungi • *Guided Reading and Study*

2. List the three categories into which scientists group protists.

   a. _____

   b. _____

   c. _____

Animal-Like Protists (pp. 75–78)

3. Circle the letter of each characteristic that animal-like protists share with animals.

   a. autotroph   b. heterotroph
   c. movement   d. unicellular

4. Another name for an animal-like protist is _____.

5. Describe how a sarcodine, such as an amoeba, gets food.

   _____

   _____

   _____

6. Circle the letter of the cell part in an ameoba that removes excess water.

   a. pseudopod   b. cilia
   c. contractile vacuole d. cell membrane

7. Is the following sentence true or false? Paramecia have more than one nucleus. _____

Match the animal-like protist with the cell part it uses for movement.

Protist   **Cell Part**

____ 8. amoeba   a. cilia

____ 9. paramecium   b. flagella

____ 10. flagellate   c. pseudopods

11. Is the following sentence true or false? Flagellates living in symbiosis always harm the animal in which they live. _____

© Pearson Education, Inc., publishing as Pearson Prentice Hall. All rights reserved.

Protists and Fungi ▪ *Guided Reading and Study*

Protists *(continued)*

12. Protozoans that are _____ feed on the cells and body fluids of their hosts.

13. Is the following sentence true or false? Protozoans that are parasites never have more than one host. _____

Plantlike Protists (pp. 79–81)

14. Plantlike protists are commonly called _____.

15. Like plants, plantlike protists are _____; most are able to use the sun's energy to make their own food.

16. Complete this table about the different types of plantlike protists.

Characteristics of Plantlike Protists

Type	Unicellular or Multicellular	Characteristics
Diatoms		
Dinoflagellates		
Euglenoids		
Red Algae		
Green Algae		
Brown Algae		

© Pearson Education, Inc., publishing as Pearson Prentice Hall. All rights reserved.

Protists and Fungi • *Guided Reading and Study*

Funguslike Protists (pp. 82–83)

17. Circle the letter of each sentence that is true about funguslike protists.

    a. Funguslike protists are heterotrophs.
    b. Funguslike protists do not have cell walls.
    c. Funguslike protists use spores to reproduce.
    d. Funguslike protists never move during their lives.

18. List the three types of funguslike protists.

    a. _____

    b. _____

    c. _____

19. Where do most water molds and downy mildews live? _____

    _____

20. Circle the letter of each place where slime molds live.

    a. dry soil   b. moist soil

    c. decaying plants   d. in animals

Protists and Fungi · *Guided Reading and Study*

Algal Blooms (pp. 84–86)

This section describes how the rapid growth of algae affects ocean water and fresh water.

Use Target Reading Skills

As you read, compare and contrast the two types of algal blooms in the table below.

Algal Blooms

Properties	Saltwater Blooms	Freshwater Blooms
Causes	Increase in nutrients or temperature	
Effects		

Saltwater Blooms (p. 85)

1. Circle the letter of each sentence that is true about saltwater algal blooms.

     a. Saltwater algal blooms are commonly called red tides.

     b. The water is red during a red tide because of toxins produced by the algae.

     c. Red tides are never any other color but red.

     d. Dinoflagellates and diatoms are two kinds of algae that often cause red tides.

2. List two conditions that often cause red tides to occur.

     a. _____

     b. _____

© Pearson Education, Inc., publishing as Pearson Prentice Hall. All rights reserved.

Protists and Fungi ▪ *Guided Reading and Study*

3. Why are red tides dangerous to people and other organisms?

_____

_____

_____

Freshwater Blooms (p. 86)

4. In a process called _____ nutrients, such as
nitrogen and phosphorus, build up in a lake or pond over time, causing
an increase in the growth of algae.

5. Complete the following flowchart to show what occurs when algae
grow rapidly in a pond or lake.

Eutrophication

Algae on the water's surface prevent _____

from reaching plants and other algae underwater. These plants

_____ and sink to the bottom.

↓

_____ that break down the remains of the dead

plants increase in number and use up all the _____

in the water.

↓

Fish and other organisms _____ without the

_____ they need to survive.

© Pearson Education, Inc., publishing as Pearson Prentice Hall. All rights reserved.

Protists and Fungi • *Guided Reading and Study*

Fungi (pp. 88–95)

This section explains what fungi are, how they get food, and their role in the environment.

Use Target Reading Skills

Before you read, preview the red headings. In the graphic organizer below, ask a what *or* how *question for each heading. As you read, write answers to your questions.*

Fungi

Question	Answer
What are fungi?	Fungi are . . .

What Are Fungi? (pp. 88–90)

1. Circle the letter before each sentence that is true about fungi.

   a. All fungi are multicellular organisms.
   b. They are eukaryotes.
   c. Most use spores to reproduce.
   d. They are autotrophs.

2. What are three examples of fungi?

   _____

   _____

   _____

© Pearson Education, Inc., publishing as Pearson Prentice Hall. All rights reserved.

Protists and Fungi · *Guided Reading and Study*

3. The cells of fungi are arranged in branching, threadlike tubes called
   _____.

4. Is the following sentence true or false? Fuzzy-looking molds that grow on food have hyphae that are packed tightly together. _____

5. Identify the structures of the mushroom shown here.

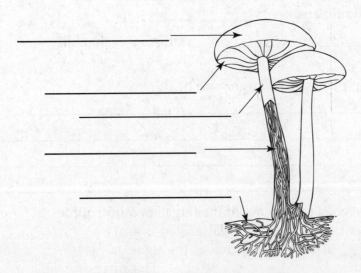

6. Describe the process by which a fungus feeds.

   _____
   _____
   _____
   _____
   _____

7. Is the following sentence true or false? Some fungi are parasites.

   _____

Reproduction in Fungi (pp. 90–91)

8. Most fungi reproduce by making _____.

9. Yeast cells reproduce asexually in a process called _____.

10. Is the following sentence true or false? Fungi reproduce sexually when growing conditions become unfavorable. _____

11. What are the three major groups of fungi?

    a. _____ b. _____

    c. _____

© Pearson Education, Inc., publishing as Pearson Prentice Hall. All rights reserved.

Protists and Fungi • *Guided Reading and Study*

Fungi *(continued)*

The Role of Fungi in Nature (pp. 92–95)

12. Fungi that are _____ break down the chemicals in dead organisms.

13. Is the following sentence true or false? Certain kinds of fungi cause diseases in plants and in humans. _____

14. Some molds produce _____, substances that kill bacteria.

15. How do some fungi help plants grow larger and healthier?

_____

_____

_____

_____

16. An organism that consists of a fungus and either algae or autotrophic bacteria that live together in a mutualistic relationship is a(n) _____. The fungus provides the algae or autotrophic bacteria with _____. The algae or autotrophic bacteria provide the fungus with _____.

© Pearson Education, Inc., publishing as Pearson Prentice Hall. All rights reserved.

Protists and Fungi · *Key Terms*

Key Terms

Match each definition on the left with the correct term on the right. Then write the number of each term in the appropriate box below. When you have filled in all the boxes, add up the numbers in each column, row, and two diagonals. The sums should be the same. Some terms may not be used.

A. Asexual reproduction in yeast

B. A temporary bulge of the cytoplasm used for feeding and movement

C. An interaction between two species in which at least one of the species benefits

D. Nutrients build up in a lake over time, causing an increase in algal growth

E. Reproductive hyphae that grow out of a fungus

F. Chemical that produces color

G. An interaction between two species in which both partners benefit

H. Hairlike projections from cells that move with a wavelike pattern

I. The rapid growth of a population of algae

1. pseudopod
2. mutualism
3. pigment
4. algal bloom
5. fruiting bodies
6. budding
7. eutrophication
8. symbiosis
9. cilia
10. spore
11. contractile vacuole
12. lichen

A	B	C	= _____
_____	_____	_____	
D	E	F	= _____
_____	_____	_____	
G	H	I	= _____
_____	_____	_____	= _____
=	=	=	
_____	_____	_____	

© Pearson Education, Inc., publishing as Pearson Prentice Hall. All rights reserved.

Name _____ Date _____ Class _____

The Plant Kingdom (pp. 104–111)

This section explains the features that plants share. It also describes what plants need to survive and how they reproduce.

Use Target Reading Skills

The first column in the chart lists Key Terms in this section. In the second column, write what you know about the Key Term. As you read the section, write a definition of the Key Term in your own words in the third column. Some examples are done for you.

Key Term	What You Know	Definition
Photosynthesis		
Tissue		
Chloroplast	*chloro* means "green"	
Vacuole		
Cuticle		Waxy, waterproof layer of a plant that reduces water loss.
Vascular tissue		
Fertilization		
Zygote		
Nonvascular plant	non means "no"	
Vascular plant		
Chlorophyll	*chloro* means "green"	
Sporophyte		
Gametophyte		

© Pearson Education, Inc., publishing as Pearson Prentice Hall. All rights reserved.

Name _____ Date _____ Class _____

Introduction to Plants · *Guided Reading and Study*

What Is a Plant? (pp. 104–105)

1. Circle the letter of each characteristic that plants share.
   a. heterotroph
   b. autotroph
   c. prokaryote
   d. eukaryote

2. Is the following sentence true or false? Plants make their own food in the process of photosynthesis. _____

3. Plant cells have a(n) _____, a boundary that surrounds the cell membrane and separates the cell from the environment.

4. Cell walls are made mostly of _____, a chemical that makes the walls rigid.

5. Label the diagram of the plant cell below.

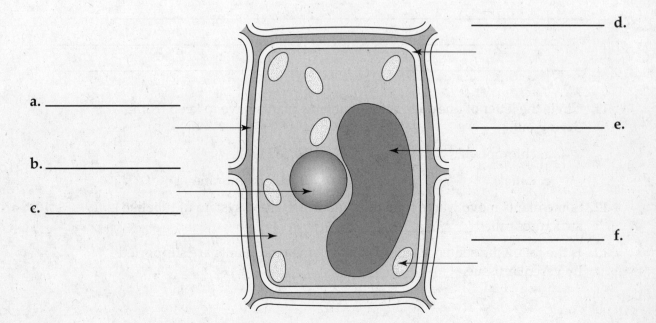

a. _____

b. _____

c. _____

d. _____

e. _____

f. _____

6. Is the following sentence true or false? Only some plants are multicellular. _____

7. A group of similar cells that perform a specific function in an organism is a(n) _____.

© Pearson Education, Inc., publishing as Pearson Prentice Hall. All rights reserved.

Name _____ Date _____ Class _____

Introduction to Plants • *Guided Reading and Study*

The Plant Kingdom *(continued)*

Adaptations for Living on Land (pp. 106–107)

8. List five things that plants must do to survive on land.

   a. _____

   b. _____

   c. _____

   d. _____

   e. _____

9. Plants living on land get water and nutrients from the
   _____ .

10. Why can a plant on land lose water and dry out?

    _____

    _____

    _____

    _____

11. Circle the letter of one adaptation that land plants have to keep from
    drying out.

    a. chlorophyll   **b.** cell wall

    c. cuticle   **d.** cell membrane

12. Some plants move water, minerals, and food with a system of tubelike
    structures called _____ .

13. Is the following sentence true or false? Some land plants are supported
    by vascular tissue. _____

© Pearson Education, Inc., publishing as Pearson Prentice Hall. All rights reserved.

Name _____ Date _____ Class _____

Introduction to Plants · *Guided Reading and Study*

14. What occurs during fertilization?

_____

_____

15. Circle the letter of the name of a fertilized egg.
  a. sporophyte
  b. gamete
  c. gametophyte
  d. zygote

Classification of Plants (pp. 108–110)

16. How do biologists learn which organisms were the ancestors of today's plants?

_____

17. A green pigment found in the chloroplasts of plants is called _____.

18. Why do biologists think that ancient green algae were the ancestors of today's plants?

_____

_____

Complex Life Cycles (pp. 110–111)

19. Plants produce spores during the _____ stage and

produce sex cells during the _____ stage.

20. Is the following sentence true or false? The sporophyte of a plant looks

the same as the gametophyte. _____

21. What are two kinds of sex cells that a gametophyte produces?
  a. _____ **b.** _____

© Pearson Education, Inc., publishing as Pearson Prentice Hall. All rights reserved.

Introduction to Plants ▪ *Guided Reading and Study*

Photosynthesis and Light (pp. 114–119)

This section explains how plants get energy from sunlight and describes what occurs during photosynthesis.

Use Target Reading Skills

Preview the figure, "The Photosynthesis Process" in the textbook. Then write two questions that you have about the diagram below. As you read, answer your questions.

The Photosynthesis Process

Q. How is sunlight involved in photosynthesis?	
A.	
Q.	
A.	

The Nature of Light (pp. 115–116)

1. Circle the letter of each sentence that is true about light.

    a. The sun is the source of energy on Earth.

    b. The light you can see is called a prism.

    c. White light is made up of red, orange, yellow, green, blue, and violet light.

    d. Shiny surfaces absorb light and dark surfaces reflect light.

2. The colors of light that make up white light are referred to as the

    _____.

3. A shirt looks red because it _____ red light.

© Pearson Education, Inc., publishing as Pearson Prentice Hall. All rights reserved.

Introduction to Plants · *Guided Reading and Study*

4. Circle the color of light that is reflected by plant leaves.

   a. green
   b. blue
   c. yellow
   d. red

5. Light is absorbed by _____ found in the chloroplasts of plant cells.

6. Circle the letter of each color of light that is absorbed by chlorophyll.

   a. green
   b. blue
   c. yellow
   d. red

7. Circle the letter of each sentence that is true about plant pigments.

   a. Accessory pigments absorb the same colors of light that chlorophyll does.
   b. Accessory pigments are always visible in plants.
   c. Accessory pigments absorb different colors of light than chlorophyll.
   d. Most accessory pigments are not visible in plants because they are masked by chlorophyll.

The Photosynthesis Process (pp. 117–119)

8. How is the light energy absorbed by plants important to photosynthesis?

   _____

   _____

   _____

9. In addition to light, what do plants need for photosynthesis?

   _____

   _____

© Pearson Education, Inc., publishing as Pearson Prentice Hall. All rights reserved.

Introduction to Plants · *Guided Reading and Study*

Photosynthesis and Light *(continued)*

10. In the diagram below, draw arrows to show which materials the plant is taking up and which materials the plant is giving off or using.

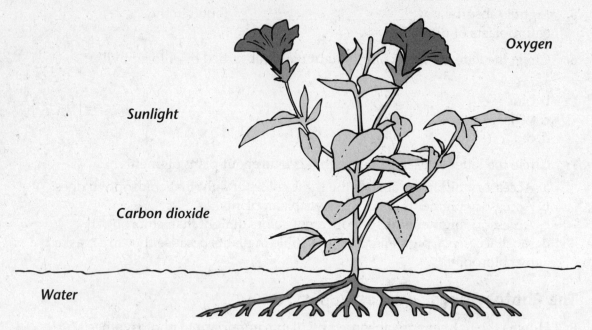

Oxygen

Sunlight

Carbon dioxide

Water

11. Write the chemical equation for the process of photosynthesis.

_____

12. What happens to excess food made by plants?

_____

_____

© Pearson Education, Inc., publishing as Pearson Prentice Hall. All rights reserved.

Name _____ Date _____ Class _____

Mosses, Liverworts, and Hornworts (pp. 122–124)

This section describes the characteristics of nonvascular plants.

Use Target Reading Skills

As you read the section, write the main idea—the biggest or most important idea—in the graphic organizer below. Then write three supporting details that give examples of the main idea.

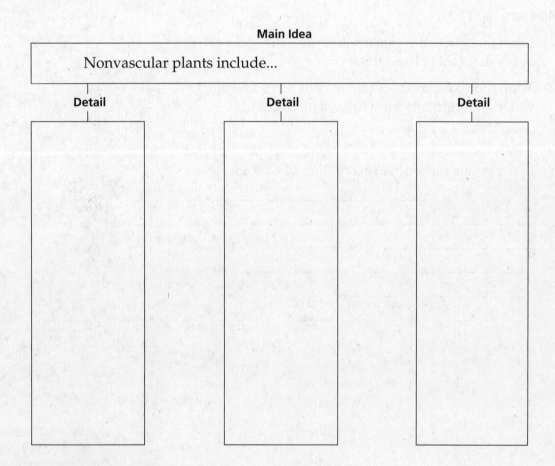

Main Idea

Nonvascular plants include...

Detail   **Detail**   **Detail**

Introduction (p. 122)

1. List two characteristics of nonvascular plants.

   a. _____

   b. _____

2. Is the following sentence true or false? Nonvascular plants can become very large and tall because of their support system. _____

© Pearson Education, Inc., publishing as Pearson Prentice Hall. All rights reserved.

Introduction to Plants • *Guided Reading and Study*

Mosses, Liverworts, and Hornworts (continued)

3. How do nonvascular plants get water?

_____

_____

4. Is the following true or false? Nonvascular plants must have water to let the sperm cells swim to the egg cells. _____

Mosses (p. 123)

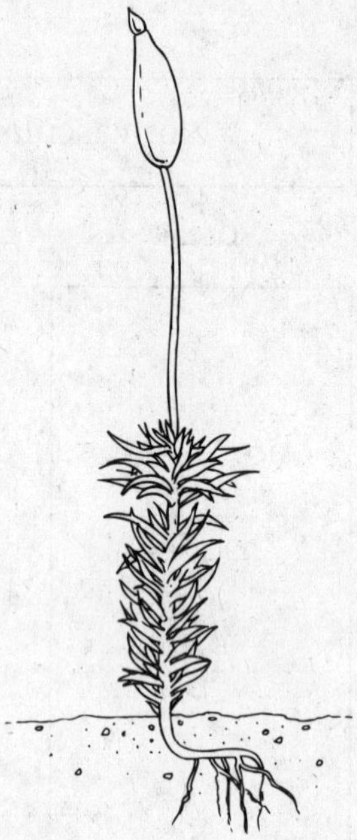

5. Label and circle the gametophyte and the sporophyte in the diagram of the moss.

6. Thin, rootlike structures that anchor moss and absorb water and nutrients from the soil are called

_____.

7. Describe the sporophyte generation of a moss.

_____

_____

_____

_____

_____

_____

© Pearson Education, Inc., publishing as Pearson Prentice Hall. All rights reserved.

Introduction to Plants • *Guided Reading and Study*

8. Circle the letter of each way people use peat moss.
   a. as food
   b. in gardening
   c. as a fuel
   d. as cloth

9. Is the following sentence true or false? Peat moss forms in bogs where dead plants do not decay, but are pressed into layers as they fall to the bottom of the bog. _____

Liverworts and Hornworts (p. 124)

10. Where are liverworts often found growing?

_____

_____

11. Is the following sentence true or false? There are more species of hornworts than there are liverworts. _____

© Pearson Education, Inc., publishing as Pearson Prentice Hall. All rights reserved.

Introduction to Plants • *Guided Reading and Study*

Ferns, Club Mosses, and Horsetails (pp. 126–129)

This section describes the characteristics of plants that have vascular tissue, but do not produce seeds.

Use Target Reading Skills

Before you read, preview the red headings. In the graphic organizer below, ask a what, how, *or* where *question for each heading. As you read, write the answers to your questions.*

Ferns, Club Mosses, and Horsetails

Question	Answer
What are the characteristics of seedless vascular plants?	Seedless vascular plants have...

Characteristics of Seedless Vascular Plants (p. 127)

1. List two characteristics that ferns, club mosses, and horsetails share.

    a. _____

    b. _____

2. Circle the letter before each sentence that is true about vascular tissue.

    a. Plants can grow tall without vascular tissue.

    b. Nonvascular plants are better suited to life on land.

    c. Vascular tissue transports water and food throughout a plant's body.

    d. Vascular tissue gives a plant strength and stability.

© Pearson Education, Inc., publishing as Pearson Prentice Hall. All rights reserved.

Introduction to Plants ▪ *Guided Reading and Study*

3. Why must ferns, club mosses, and horsetails grow in moist surroundings?

_____

_____

_____

Ferns (p. 128)

4. Is the following sentence true or false? Ferns are small plants that can only grow low to the ground. _____

5. The stems of most ferns are located _____. Leaves grow _____ from the top side of the stems, and roots grow _____ from the bottom of the stems.

6. Why are the developing leaves in many ferns called fiddleheads?

_____

_____

7. Circle the letter of each sentence that is true about the function of a fern's roots.
   a. Roots anchor the fern to the ground.
   b. Roots keep the fern from losing water.
   c. Roots produce spores.
   d. Roots absorb water and nutrients from the soil.

© Pearson Education, Inc., publishing as Pearson Prentice Hall. All rights reserved.

Ferns, Club Mosses, and Horsetails (continued)

8. Fern leaves are called _____.

9. What is the function of the cuticle on the upper surface of fern leaves?

_____

10. Circle the letter of each sentence that is true about reproduction in ferns.

    a. The familiar fern plant with its large fronds is the gametophyte stage.
    b. Spores develop in spore cases on the underside of mature fronds.
    c. Wind and water carry released spores great distances.
    d. Spores will grow into gametophytes in dry, sunny soil.

Club Mosses and Horsetails (p. 129)

11. How are club mosses and horsetails similar to ferns?

_____

_____

_____

12. Circle the letter before each sentence that is true about club mosses and horsetails.

    a. There are thousands of different species of club mosses and horsetails.
    b. Club mosses usually grow in moist woodlands and near streams.
    c. Club mosses have jointed stems with long, needlelike branches that grow in a circle around each joint.
    d. Horsetail stems contain silica, a gritty substance also found in sand.

© Pearson Education, Inc., publishing as Pearson Prentice Hall. All rights reserved.

Key Terms

Use the clues to fill in the blanks with Key Terms from the chapter. Then put the numbered letters in the correct spaces to find the hidden message.

| **Clues** | **Key Terms** |

Stage in which plant produces
spores

— — — — — — — — — — —
1   2   3   4   5

Fern leaf

— — — — —
6   7   8   9

Group of cells that has a
specific job

— — — — — —
10   11   12   13

Rootlike structure that
anchors moss

— — — — — —
14   15   16

Type of wetland

— — —
17

Saclike storage area in a
plant cell

— — — — — — —
18   19   20   21   22

Stage in which plant
produces sex cells

— — — — — — — — — —
   23   24   25   26   27

Layer of dead mosses
compressed at the bottom
of a bog

— — — —
   28   29   30

Mosses and liverworts are
_____ plants

— — — — — — — — —
31   32   33   34   35   36   37   38

Green pigment

— — — — — — — — — —
   39   40   41

Hidden Message

— — — — — — — —   — — — — — — — — — —
18 23 12 35 13 21 37 14   3 39 33 8 25 34   29 38 5

— — — — — —   — — — — — —   — — — — — —
17 22 4 26 24 7   1 20 15 10 28 9   30 40   41 11 6 27

— — — — — — .
2 32   36 19 31 16

© Pearson Education, Inc., publishing as Pearson Prentice Hall. All rights reserved.

Seed Plants · *Guided Reading and Study*

The Characteristics of Seed Plants (pp. 136–145)

This section tells about the characteristics of seed plants. It also describes the parts of a seed and the functions of leaves, stems, and roots.

Use Target Reading Skills

As you read, make an outline about seed plants that you can use for review. Use the red headings for the main topics and blue headings for the supporting ideas.

The Characteristics of Seed Plants
I. What is a Seed Plant?
A. Vascular Tissue
B.
II. How Seeds Become New Plants
A.
B.
C.

What Is a Seed Plant? (pp. 136–137)

1. Circle the letter of each sentence that is true about seed plants.

    a. Seedless plants outnumber seed plants.
    b. Seed plants do not have vascular tissue.
    c. Seed plants use seeds to reproduce.
    d. All seed plants have roots, leaves, and stems.

2. In seed plants, the plants that you see are in the _____ stage of the life cycle. The _____ stage is microscopic.

3. In what two ways does vascular tissue help seed plants to live on land?

    a. _____

    b. _____

4. Circle the letter of the vascular tissue through which food moves.
    a. xylem
    b. phloem
    c. roots
    d. stems

© Pearson Education, Inc., publishing as Pearson Prentice Hall. All rights reserved.

Seed Plants · *Guided Reading and Study*

5. Circle the letter of the vascular tissue through which water moves.

   a. xylem

   b. phloem

   c. roots

   d. stems

6. Food made in the plant's _____ travels to the roots and stems.

7. Water and nutrients absorbed by the plant's _____ travel to the stems and leaves.

8. What is a seed?

   _____

   _____

9. Is the following sentence true or false? Pollen delivers sperm cells directly near the eggs. _____

How Seeds Become New Plants (pp. 138–140)

Match the part of the seed with its function.

Seed Part	Function
____ 10. embryo	**a.** Keeps the seed from drying out
____ 11. cotyledon	**b.** Young plant that develops from the fertilized egg
____ 12. seed coat	**c.** A seed leaf that sometimes stores food

13. What do seeds need to develop into a new plant?

   _____

   _____

14. Is the following sentence true or false? Seeds can begin to grow in any place they land. _____

© Pearson Education, Inc., publishing as Pearson Prentice Hall. All rights reserved.

Name _____ Date _____ Class _____

The Characteristics of Seed Plants (continued)

15. Complete the concept map to show ways that seeds are dispersed.

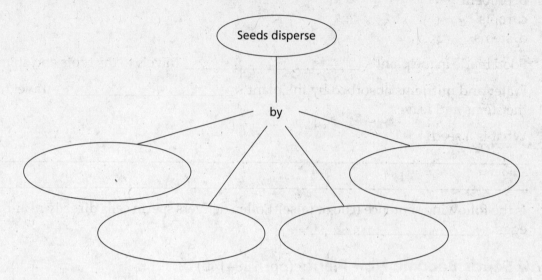

16. What is germination?

_____

_____

17. Circle the letter before each sentence that is true about germination.

   a. All seeds germinate immediately after they are dispersed.
   b. The embryo uses its stored food to begin to grow.
   c. First, the embryo's leaves and stem grow upward.
   d. Seeds that are dispersed far away from the parent have a better chance of survival.

Roots (pp. 140–142)

18. List three functions of roots.

   a. _____

   b. _____

   c. _____

© Pearson Education, Inc., publishing as Pearson Prentice Hall. All rights reserved.

19. Look at the two types of root systems illustrated below. Label the roots
    as taproot or fibrous roots.

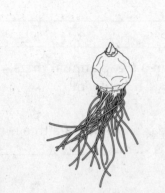

a. _____   b. _____
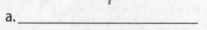

Match the root structure with its function.

Root Structure	Function
____ 20. root cap	a. Moves food to the roots and other parts of plant
____ 21. root hairs	b. Protects the root from injury during growth
____ 22. phloem	c. Moves water and minerals to the stems and leaves
____ 23. xylem	d. Increase the amount of water and minerals absorbed by the root

24. Circle the letter of the cell layer that produces new phloem and xylem.
    a. heartwood
    b. sapwood
    c. bark
    d. cambium

Stems (pp. 142–143)

25. List three functions of stems.

    a. _____

    b. _____

    c. _____

© Pearson Education, Inc., publishing as Pearson Prentice Hall. All rights reserved.

Name _____ Date _____ Class _____

The Characteristics of Seed Plants (continued)

26. Is the following sentence true or false? Herbaceous stems are hard and rigid and have an outer layer called bark. _____

27. What is heartwood?

_____

_____

28. Circle the letter before the tissue that makes up a tree's annual rings.
   a. xylem   **b.** phloem
   c. cambium   **d.** bark

29. Is the following sentence true or false? One year's growth of a tree is represented by one pair of light and dark rings in the tree's stem. _____

Leaves (pp. 144–145)

30. What role do leaves play in a plant?

_____

_____

_____

Match the leaf part with its function.

Leaf Part	Function
____ **31.** cuticle	**a.** Widely spaced cells allow carbon dioxide and oxygen to pass in and out of the leaf.
____ **32.** xylem	
____ **33.** phloem	**b.** Carries water from the roots to the leaves
____ **34.** stomata	**c.** Waxy, waterproof coating that covers a leaf's surface
____ **35.** lower leaf cells	**d.** Contain the most chloroplasts
____ **36.** upper leaf cells	**e.** Carries food made in the leaves to the rest of the plant
	f. Tiny pores that open and close to let carbon dioxide in and water vapor and oxygen out

37. Is the following sentence true or false? The tightly packed cells of the upper leaf enable the leaf to trap the energy in sunlight. _____

38. The process by which water evaporates from a plant's leaves is called _____ .

39. Is the following sentence true or false? Stomata close to keep the plant from losing water. _____

© Pearson Education, Inc., publishing as Pearson Prentice Hall. All rights reserved.

Seed Plants · *Guided Reading and Study*

Gymnosperms (pp. 146–150)

This section gives examples of the group of seed plants known as gymnosperms and describes their features and how they reproduce.

Use Target Reading Skills

Before you read, preview the figure, The Life Cycle of a Gymnosperm, in the textbook. Then write two questions that you have about the diagram in the graphic organizer below. As you read, answer your questions.

The Life Cycle of a Gymnosperm
Q. How does gymnosperm pollination occur?
A.
Q.
A.

What Are Gymnosperms? (pp. 146–147)

1. What is a gymnosperm?

   _____

   _____

2. Is the following sentence true or false? Gymnosperms have seeds that are not enclosed by a fruit. _____

© Pearson Education, Inc., publishing as Pearson Prentice Hall. All rights reserved.

Name _____ Date _____ Class _____

Seed Plants · *Guided Reading and Study*

Gymnosperms *(continued)*

3. Is the following sentence true or false? Gymnosperms are the oldest type of seed plant. _____

Match the gymnosperms with their features. Some gymnosperms may be used more than once.

Features

____ 4. Only one species exists today.

____ 5. They are the largest group of gymnosperms.

____ 6. These plants live in hot deserts and in tropical rain forests.

____ 7. They grow in tropical and subtropical areas.

____ 8. Most keep their needles year round.

____ 9. These plants look like palm trees with giant cones.

____ 10. Often planted along city streets because they tolerate air pollution.

Gymnosperms

a. cycads

b. ginkgoes

c. gnetophytes

d. conifers

Reproduction in Gymnosperms (pp. 148–149)

11. Most gymnosperms have reproductive structures called

_____.

12. Is the following sentence true or false? Male cones contain ovules at the base of each scale. _____

13. _____ groups of gymnosperms exist today.

14. A structure that contains an egg cell is a(n) _____.

15. What happens during pollination?

_____

_____

© Pearson Education, Inc., publishing as Pearson Prentice Hall. All rights reserved.

16. Is the following sentence true or false? In gymnosperms, wind often carries the pollen from the male cones to the female cones.

_____

17. Complete the cycle diagram showing the steps in the reproduction of gymnosperms.

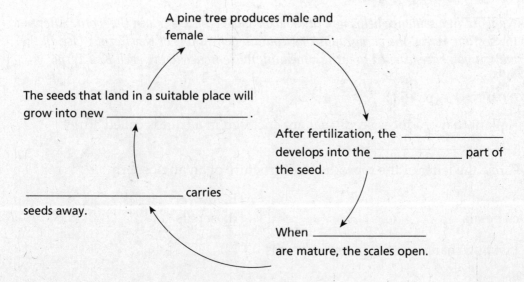

A pine tree produces male and female _____ .

The seeds that land in a suitable place will grow into new _____ .

After fertilization, the _____ develops into the _____ part of the seed.

_____ carries seeds away.

When _____ are mature, the scales open.

Gymnosperms in Everyday Life (p. 150)

18. Circle the letter of each product that conifers provide.

    a. fruit
    b. paper
    c. turpentine
    d. cotton fibers

19. Is the following sentence true or false? When adult trees in managed forests are cut down, no trees are planted to replace them.

_____

© Pearson Education, Inc., publishing as Pearson Prentice Hall. All rights reserved.

Seed Plants • *Guided Reading and Study*

Angiosperms (pp. 151–157)

This section describes the type of seed plants that produce fruit and their life cycle. It also explains the difference between two groups of plants that produce different kinds of seeds.

Use Target Reading Skills

Using a word in a sentence helps you think about how best to explain the word. After you read the section, reread the paragraphs that contain definitions of Key Terms. Use all the information you have learned to write a meaningful sentence using each Key Term.

Introduction (p. 151)

1. A plant that produces seeds that are enclosed in a fruit is called a(n) _____ .

2. Circle the letter of the reproductive structure of an angiosperm.

    a. seed   b. flower
    c. petals   d. sepals

3. List two characteristics of angiosperms.

    a. _____

    b. _____

The Structure of Flowers (pp. 152–153)

Match the parts of the flower with their function.

Function	Flower Parts
____ 4. Male reproductive parts	a. petals
	b. sepals
____ 5. Protect the developing flower	c. stamens
	d. pistils
____ 6. Female reproductive parts	
____ 7. Colorful structures that attract pollinators	

© Pearson Education, Inc., publishing as Pearson Prentice Hall. All rights reserved.

Seed Plants • *Guided Reading and Study*

8. Label the parts of the flower in this diagram.

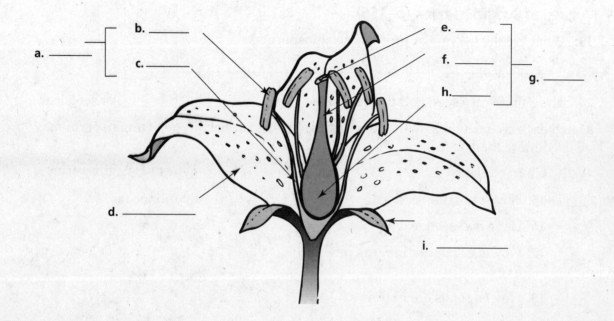

Reproduction in Angiosperms (pp. 154–155)

9. When a flower is pollinated, a grain of pollen falls on a(n)
    _____.

10. In what part of the flower do the sperm cell and the egg cell join
    together?

    _____

11. Is the following sentence true or false? All angiosperms rely on wind for
    pollination. _____

12. Describe how animals help to pollinate flowers.

    _____

    _____

    _____

    _____

© Pearson Education, Inc., publishing as Pearson Prentice Hall. All rights reserved.

Name _____ Date _____ Class _____

Seed Plants • *Guided Reading and Study*

Angiosperms (continued)

Types of Angiosperms (p. 156)

13. What are the two major groups of angiosperms?

    a._____ b._____

14. The embryo in a seed gets food from the _____, or seed leaf.

Match each characteristic with the type of angiosperm. Each type of angiosperm may be used more than once.

Characteristics	Types of Angiosperms
_____ 15. Have only one seed leaf	**a.** monocots
_____ 16. Have two seed leaves	**b.** dicots
_____ 17. Flower petals are in fours or fives.	
_____ 18. Flower petals are in threes.	
_____ 19. Leaves are wide with branching veins.	
_____ 20. Leaves are narrow with parallel veins.	
_____ 21. Roses, violets, and oak trees are examples.	
_____ 22. Corn, wheat, and tulips are examples.	

Angiosperms in Everyday Life (p. 157)

23. Circle the letter of each product made from angiosperms.
    a. furniture
    b. clothing
    c. turpentine
    d. steel

24. Is the following sentence true or false? Medicines, such as digitalis, come from angiosperms. _____

© Pearson Education, Inc., publishing as Pearson Prentice Hall. All rights reserved.

Name _____ Date _____ Class _____

Plant Responses and Growth (pp. 160–164)

This section explains how plants respond to stimuli in their environment. It also describes the role of plant hormones and the life spans of flowering seed plants.

Use Target Reading Skills

As you read through the paragraphs under the heading Hormones and Tropisms, identify four effects of plant hormones. Write the information in the graphic organizer below.

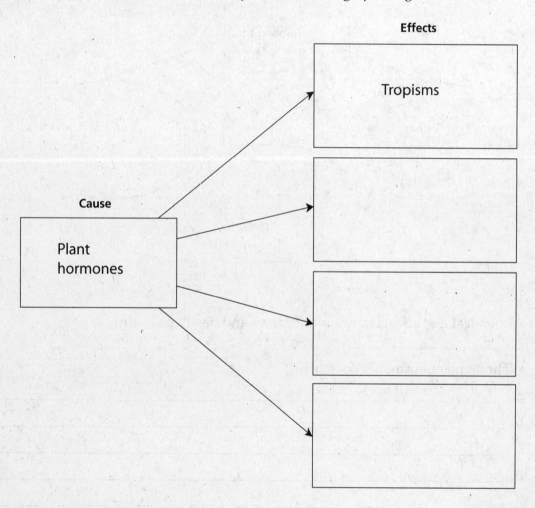

Tropisms (pp. 160–161)

1. What is a tropism?

   _____

   _____

2. Is the following sentence true or false? If a plant grows toward the stimulus, it shows a negative tropism. _____

© Pearson Education, Inc., publishing as Pearson Prentice Hall. All rights reserved.

Plant Responses and Growth (continued)

3. Complete the concept map to show three stimuli to which plants respond.

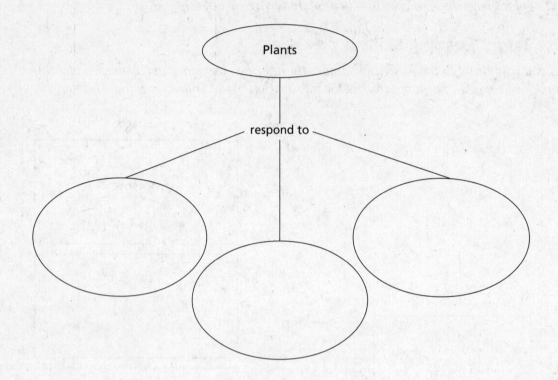

4. A chemical that affects how a plant grows and develops is a(n)
   _____.

5. What do plant hormones control?

   a. _____

   b. _____

   c. _____

   d. _____

   e. _____

6. Auxin is a plant hormone that _____ the rate at
   which a plant's cells grow.

7. Describe how auxin controls a plant's response to light.

   _____

   _____

   _____

   _____

   _____

© Pearson Education, Inc., publishing as Pearson Prentice Hall. All rights reserved.

Seed Plants • *Guided Reading and Study*

Seasonal Changes (pp. 162–163)

8. What determines the time of flowering in many plants?

_____

_____

9. What happens to a plant during dormancy?

_____

_____

Life Spans of Angiosperms (p. 164)

10. Circle the letter of the flowering plants that complete a life cycle within one growing season.

    a. perennials   **b.** biennials

    c. annuals   **d.** centennials

11. Is the following sentence true or false? Most annuals have woody stems.

_____

12. Circle the letter of each sentence that is true about biennials.

    a. Biennials complete their life cycle in two years.

    b. In the first year, biennials produce seeds and flowers.

    c. In the second year, biennials germinate and grow roots.

    d. Once the flower produces seeds, the biennial dies.

13. How long is the life cycle of a perennial?

_____

_____

14. Circle the letter of the plant that is a perennial.

    a. parsley   **b.** peony

    c. cucumber   **d.** petunia

© Pearson Education, Inc., publishing as Pearson Prentice Hall. All rights reserved.

Seed Plants · *Guided Reading and Study*

Feeding the World (pp. 165–167)

This section describes different ways farmers can produce more crops.

Use Target Reading Skills

As you read the section, write the main idea in the graphic organizer below. Then write three supporting details that give examples of the main idea.

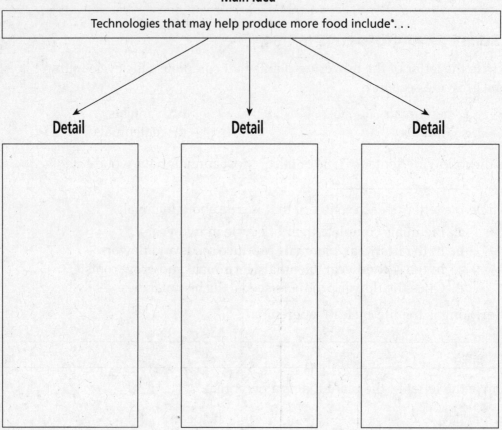

Main Idea

Technologies that may help produce more food include*. . .

Detail   **Detail**   **Detail**

Introduction (p. 165)

1. List three ways scientists and farmers are working to grow enough food to feed the growing population of people.

    a. _____

    _____

    b. _____

    _____

    c. _____

    _____

© Pearson Education, Inc., publishing as Pearson Prentice Hall. All rights reserved.

Seed Plants · *Guided Reading and Study*

Precision Farming (p. 166)

2. Is the following sentence true or false? In precision farming, farmers know how much water and fertilizer different fields need.
   _____

3. Complete the flowchart to show the process of precision farming.

Precision Farming

A(n) _____ takes images of a farmer's field.

↓

A computer analyzes the images to determine the makeup of the _____ in different fields on the farm.

↓

The computer prepares a(n)_____ and _____ plan for each field.

4. List three ways in which precision farming benefits farmers.
   a. _____ b. _____

   c. _____

5. Is the following sentence true or false? Precision farming benefits the environment by using more fertilizer than the soil needs.
   _____

© Pearson Education, Inc., publishing as Pearson Prentice Hall. All rights reserved.

Name _____ Date _____ Class _____

Feeding the World (continued)

Hydroponics (p. 166)

6. What is hydroponics?

_____

_____

_____

7. Is the following sentence true or false? Hydroponics can be used to grow crops in places with poor soil. _____

Engineering Better Plants (p. 167)

8. What are four major sources of food for people?

_____

_____

9. Is the following sentence true or false? Farmers can easily feed more people without increasing the production of crops.

_____

10. What two challenges do farmers face in producing more crops?

    a. _____

    b. _____

11. Scientists change an organism's genetic material to produce an organism with useful qualities in the process of _____.

© Pearson Education, Inc., publishing as Pearson Prentice Hall. All rights reserved.

Seed Plants · *Key Terms*

Key Terms

How fast can you solve this crossword puzzle? You'll need to use what you've learned about seed plants. Go!

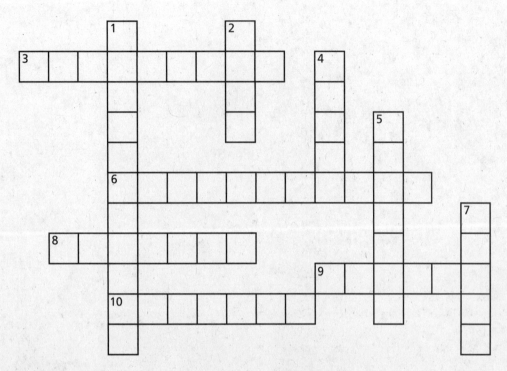

Clues down

1. A method by which plants are grown in solutions of nutrients instead of soil
2. The reproductive structure in gymnosperms
4. A ripened ovary that encloses one or more seeds
5. A plant's growth response
7. Vascular tissue through which water and minerals travel

Clues across

3. Seed leaf in which food is stored
6. The transfer of pollen from a male structure to a female structure
8. Angiosperms with only one seed leaf
9. The female part of a flower
10. Layer of cells that divide to produce new phloem and xylem

© Pearson Education, Inc., publishing as Pearson Prentice Hall. All rights reserved.